THE URBANA FREE LIBRARY

3 1230 00959 6111

D1369598

DISCARDED BY THE URBANA FREE LIBRARY

The Urbana Free Library

To renew: call **217-367-4057**
or go to **urbanafreelibrary.org**
and select **My Account**

The **Sophia Day**® Creative Team-
Megan Johnson, Stephanie Strouse,
Kayla Pearson, Timothy Zowada, Mel Sauder

© 2018 MVP Kids Media, LLC, all rights reserved

No part of this publication may be reproduced in whole or in part
by any mechanical, photographic or electronic process, or in the
form of any audio or video recording nor may it be stored in a
retrieval system or transmitted in any form or by any means now
known or hereafter invented or otherwise copied for public or
private use without the written permission of MVP Kids Media, LLC.
For more information regarding permission, visit our website at
www.MVPKidsMedia.com.

Published and Distributed by MVP Kids Media, LLC
Mesa, Arizona, USA
Printed by RR Donnelley Asia Printing Solutions, Ltd
Dongguan City, Guangdong Province, China
DOM June 2018, Job # 02-003-01

help**me**
UNDERSTAND ™

Feeling **Failure** &
Learning **Success** ™

REAL
mvpkids®

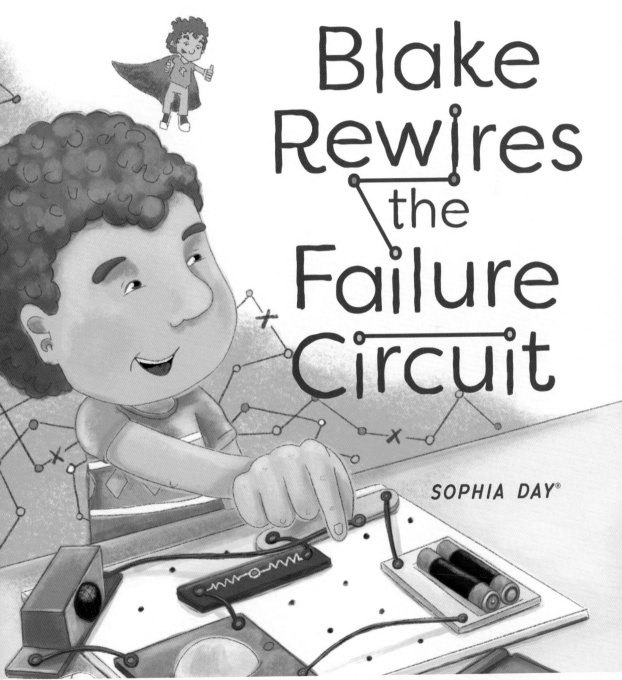

Blake
Rewires
the
Failure
Circuit

SOPHIA DAY®

Written by Megan Johnson   *Illustrated by* Stephanie Strouse

The whole school was *buzzing* with talk about the upcoming science fair. Blake *couldn't wait* to get the details from his teacher!

He listened carefully as Mrs. Hall began to explain. "I know you all want to make a flashy project, but remember that you will also be graded on how you show your process. I want to see how you learn through your project, not just the end result."

Homework
Chapter 3
Writing
Alexander Plains Elementary
Science Fair
Saturday
Doors open at 9AM
Have
The prize is in the Process

After school, Blake's mind was so full of ideas he didn't even notice his mom in the pickup line.

"Come on,
Blake,
Mom is here."

Blake lost his train of thought.

"Annie! You made me forget my best idea!"
he fussed at his sister.

"*That's it!* I'll make an alarm for my room
so Annie can't *interrupt* me," he thought.

When he got home, Blake borrowed his brother's circuit kit to make his 'Annie Alarm.'

"I can't find the instructions. Hold on, I'll check the closet," Jackson said.

"No thanks," said Blake as he started snapping parts together. He didn't know what some of the pieces did, but he put them on anyway.

"This is fun,"

he thought.

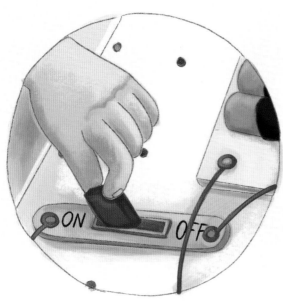

He flipped the switch.
Nothing happened.

Blake sighed. He moved a few things and tried again.
Nothing happened.

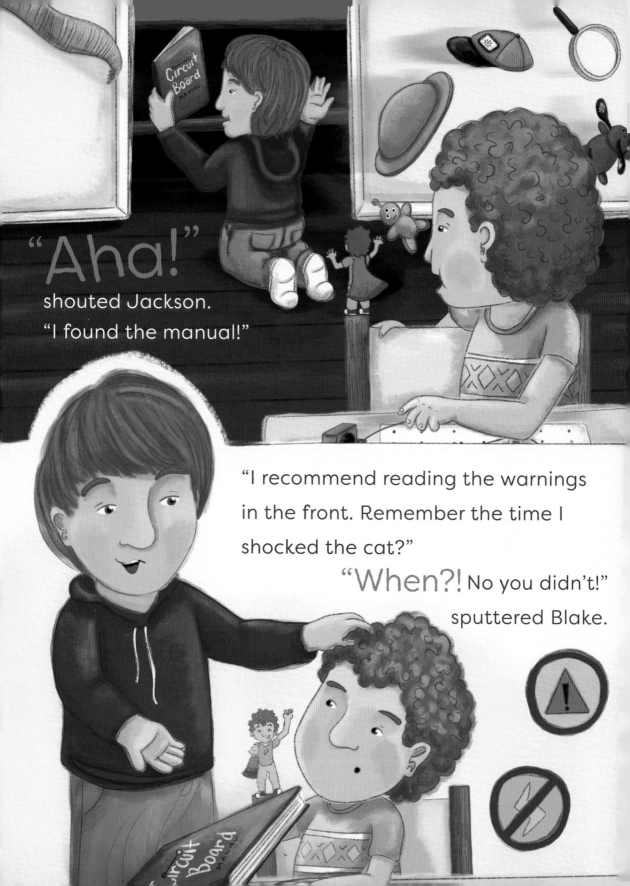

"Aha!" shouted Jackson. "I found the manual!"

"I recommend reading the warnings in the front. Remember the time I shocked the cat?"

"When?! No you didn't!" sputtered Blake.

"Just kidding, bro. But really, *read the instructions.*"

Blake flipped through the pages and found the motion detector alarm. He started moving pieces around to look like the picture, but it was overwhelming.

He just wanted the circuit to do *something*, so he quickly connected a wire across the battery pack to see what would happen.

Nothing! *Nothing* happened!

"This is **too** hard. I can't do this.
I'm going to **fail** the science project!"
A current of negative thoughts ran through his mind.

He flopped his head
back in defeat.
"I'm a failure,"
he groaned.

"Don't talk about my
son that way!"
a voice answered.

Blake saw his dad as if he were hanging from the ceiling.
"You won't get anything done right if your thinking is wrong.
You need to think positively."

"I give up!"

Blake exclaimed.
He sat up and
pushed the circuit
board aside.

"If you give up, you'll never know if you could succeed. But if you keep going and work hard, I believe you can do it! Tell me what you've tried so far."

Blake showed Dad the picture of the motion detector alarm.

"Oh wow!" exclaimed Dad. "This is an advanced project, number *86* in the manual! You're so excited that you've missed the earlier projects. If you **start at the beginning** you'll understand better."

"But I don't want to sta[rt] with the light switch ar[d] the doorbell. Jackson says those are *baby* projects." Blake folded h[is] arms in defiance. "I want to do somethin[g] *cool.*"

"First you need to understand how all the pieces work,

then you can build the more advanced projects,

and even experiment on your own,"

Dad insisted. "When you want to succeed with something new, you need to **start at the**..."

Dad started sniffing and looking around.

They turned and saw a piece of paper **smoking** on top of the circuit board!

Dad quickly picked up the paper and disconnected the circuit from the battery pack.

He gave a laugh. "Well, it looks like you made something after all!"

"But how did that happen?!" Blake asked. "I was just messing around and it wasn't doing anything.

"Hold on there. Let's **reframe** that thought," said Dad seriously.

"What do you mean '**reframe**'?" replied Blake.

"Well," said Dad, "your project started smoking and you think it's a bad thing. So imagine a picture of your smoking circuit board with a caption reading, 'Failure Project Causes House Fire'. What kind of frame would the picture have around it?"

Failure Project Causes House Fire

"An ugly, burnt black one,"

Blake said with a grin.

"Now, imagine that we take off that frame
and put on a **new one**. The new frame is shiny
and important-looking, like a trophy."

"A trophy?" Blake questioned.

"I don't understand," answered Blake.

"You didn't think you had done anything, but you actually made a short circuit...

"If you don't **start at the beginning** and push through the resistance, or challenges, *you won't accomplish what you set out to do.* Just like how your alarm didn't make a sound."

"Using shortcuts can create disasters!" laughed Blake.

"When you want to accomplish something, you need to **start at the beginning**. You don't want to miss something important by believing you know more than you do. A **successful** person is *committed to learning*."

Blake giggled.
"Even if there's resistance!"

Blake began to understand why the frame would look like a trophy. He felt good that he had learned something about circuits, even if he did learn it the hard way. It was the first step of his process in creating his project.

He remembered what
Mrs. Hall said about learning.
He would need a picture of this
for his presentation board!

Dad handed the manual to Blake, and they read the warnings together.

#1

Together, they built the light switch.

#2

Dad watched while Blake built the doorbell on his own.

As he did more projects, Blake began to understand how different resistors affected each other. He was careful not to make a short circuit again! He wanted to do this the right way, even if it took longer.

Blake worked step by step through each project. It got faster and easier the more he worked.

"You worked right through dinner!" Mom exclaimed as she set a tray of food on his bed.

"I was too excited to stop," explained Blake. "But look! I've got it now. Wave your hand here."

Mom waved her hand over a sensor and the alarm blared so loudly it startled her.

"The Sister-Away Alarm!"
Blake said with pride.
"All the boys at school will want one."

"Oh!" Mom couldn't hide her surprise. "I'm proud of your hard work, but that title will make your sister feel unloved. **True success is using our abilities to** help others**, not hurt them.** Make sure you're putting your efforts into the right purpose."

Mom went back downstairs and Blake got into bed. He began to think about how he ***didn't*** really want to hurt his sister. He decided he would use his project to help Annie somehow.

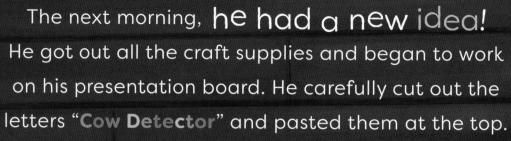

The next morning, he had a new idea!
He got out all the craft supplies and began to work
on his presentation board. He carefully cut out the
letters "Cow Detector" and pasted them at the top.

Annie loves the cows on their farm and she was always looking out the window to see if they were in the nearby pasture.

Blake's idea was to make it so his alarm would sound if a cow walked nearby. Then, she wouldn't have to always be looking!

Blake surprised Annie by practicing his presentation for her that night. She was so happy!

The day came for the science fair and Blake proudly presented his project.

There was just one problem. Every time someone walked by, the alarm sounded. It was *so loud* it was **disrupting** the entire science fair!

wheeooo wheeooooo!

Blake thought quickly about how he could **fix the problem.** He snapped out the alarm piece and traded it for the light.

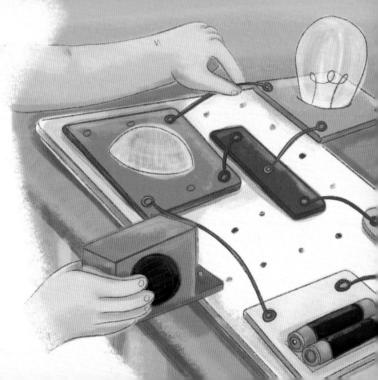

Now, when someone walked by, the light turned on instead. Blake **felt so** proud **of himself.** Mrs. Hall was very impressed!

Blake was having **so much fun** presenting his project that he didn't realize when awards were being called.

Suddenly, he heard his name.

"Blake James has earned the award for **Best Process!** Thank you, Blake, for showing us how you learned so much about electronics!"

Everyone clapped and cheered as he received his medal.

"I want to thank my sister, Annie, for inspiring my project," Blake said. "I found out that even **failure** can turn into **success** if you learn from it. It feels really good to use your talents to **help others**."

You tried so hard. You worked all day.
It's nothing but a mess.
You feel like such a failure,
but you can choose success.

Take a step back, evaluate
your process for a while.
Did you start at the beginning,
or jump ahead a mile?

Shortcuts, like short circuits,
will always let you down.
Work hard through the resistance,
and your hope will turn around.

Also featuring...

CHRISTOPHER JAMES
"Dad"

HANNAH JAMES
"Mom"

JACKSON JAMES
Brother

"PROCESS-MAN"
Can you find Blake's imaginary
sidekick throughout the book?

YONG CHEN

LEO RUSSO

FRANKIE RUSSO

JULIA ROJAS

GABBY GONZALEZ

ANNIE JAMES

AANYA PATEL

BLAKE JAMES

SARAH COHEN-GOLDSTEIN